CENTRAL AND SOUTH AMERICA

Cotopaxi, a volcano in Ecuador

The World in Maps

CENTRAL AND SOUTH AMERICA

Martyn Bramwell

Lerner Publications Company • Minneapolis

**First American edition published in 2000
by Lerner Publications Company**

© 2000 by Graham Beehag Books

Lerner Publications Company
A division of Lerner Publishing Group
241 First Avenue North
Minneapolis, MN 55401 U.S.A.

Website address: www.lernerbooks.com

Library of Congress Cataloging-in-Publication Data

Bramwell, Martyn.
    Central and South America / by Martyn Bramwell
      p. cm. — (The world in maps)
    Includes index.
    Summary: Provides information about the location, topography, climate, population, industries, languages, and currency of the Central and South American countries.
    ISBN 0-8225-2912-2 (lib. bdg.)
  1. Central America—Geography—Juvenile literature. 2. Central America—Maps for children. 3. South America—Geography—Juvenile literature.
4. South America—Maps for children. [1. Central America—Maps.
2. South America—Maps.] I. Title. II. Series: Bramwell, Martyn, The world in maps.
F1428.5 B73 2000
 917.28—dc21   99-006953

Printed in Singapore by Tat Wei Printing Packaging Pte Ltd
Bound in the United States of America
1 2 3 4 5 6 – OS – 05 04 03 02 01 00

Picture credits
Page 9 Inguat
Pages 14-15 courtesy of IPA
Page 19 Spacecharts

CONTENTS

CENTRAL AND SOUTH AMERICA

Seven countries—Belize, Guatemala, Honduras, El Salvador, Nicaragua, Costa Rica, and Panama—occupy the **isthmus** of Central America, a narrow strip of land joining North and South America. A total land area of 201,000 square miles supports about 35 million people. A volcanic mountain chain stretches 800 miles along the west side of the isthmus from Mexico to Panama, with peaks rising to 12,000 feet. Lowland plains of dense rain forest cover the eastern coast, which is frequently struck by hurricanes that sweep in from the Caribbean Sea.

The Mayan civilization, which had developed great cultural and economic advances, occupied part of Mexico and Central America for 1,500 years. Spanish invaders conquered this remarkable people in the 1520s and ruled Central America for 300 years. In 1823 five of the countries merged into a **federation** but disbanded in 1838. In the intervening years, Central America has suffered bitter conflicts between rich and poor and a succession of military dictatorships, revolutions, and wars.

The continent of South America stretches 4,600 miles from north to south and 3,200 miles from west to east. It covers an area of 6,898,579 square miles and has a population of more than 339 million. The Andes—the world's longest mountain chain—and the world's mightiest river, the Amazon, dominate the landscape. South America's climate and vegetation zones range from the rain forests of Brazil, through **savanna** and scrub in Paraguay and northern Argentina, to Chile's Atacama Desert—the driest place on earth.

The continent is rich in mineral resources. Exports include iron ore, manganese, copper, silver, mercury, gold, and emeralds, as well as the nitrates and phosphates used to make fertilizers. South America has very little coal, which has limited heavy industrialization in most countries. Oil and hydroelectric power are the primary sources of energy. South America exports hardwoods, beef, coffee, maize, cacao beans, cotton, and fresh fruits and vegetables, mostly to the United States.

Sugarloaf Mountain (Pão de Açúcar) is a towering rock landmark rising 1,300 feet above the blue waters of Guanabara Bay, Rio de Janeiro. Visitors who take the six minute cable-car ride to the top enjoy spectacular views of the city.

Belize and Guatemala

Belize

Status:	Constitutional Monarchy and Parliamentary Democracy
Area:	8,865 square miles
Population:	200,000
Capital:	Belmopan
Languages:	English, Spanish, Mayan
Currency:	Belize dollar (100 cents)

This former British colony changed its name from British Honduras to Belize in 1973 and became a fully independent nation in 1981. British troops remained in Belize until 1994 as protection from a possible invasion by neighboring Guatemala. The troops were withdrawn when Guatemala recognized Belize as a **sovereign state.**

Belize is a small country with forest-covered mountains in the south and patchy savanna and forest in the north, dotted with lakes and marshes. The country has a swampy coastal plain, and the **coral reef** that lies offshore is the world's second longest after Australia's Great Barrier Reef. More than half the population lives along the coast, 50,000 of them in Belize City, the former capital. In 1970 Belizeans built a new capital city, Belmopan, 50 miles inland—safe from the hurricanes that frequently hit the coast.

Belize City is the country's principal port, exporting tropical hardwoods, coconuts, bananas, sugarcane, and fresh fish and lobsters from the local fisheries—products account-ing for 65 percent of Belize's foreign trade. Tourism continues its rapid expansion, contributing to the country's **foreign exchange.** To lessen tourism's impact, the government has set aside some coastal land as conservation areas to protect the fragile mangrove forests and reefs from hotel and road construction and other developments.

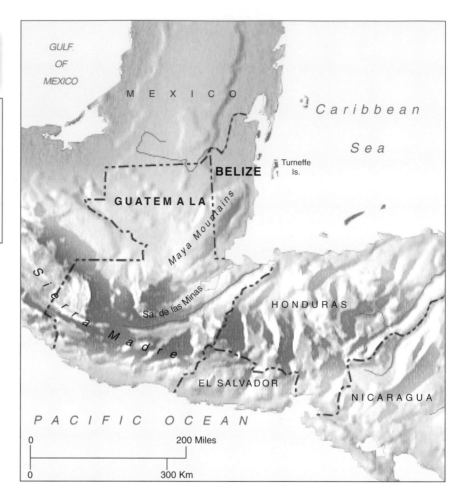

A bunch of bananas ripen on a young banana "tree"—which is not actually a tree at all. The plant is a giant herb, and the trunk consists entirely of tightly wrapped leaves.

Guatemala

Status:	Republic
Area:	42,042 square miles
Population:	12.3 million
Capital:	Guatemala City
Languages:	Spanish, Amerindian languages
Currency:	Quetzal (100 centavos)

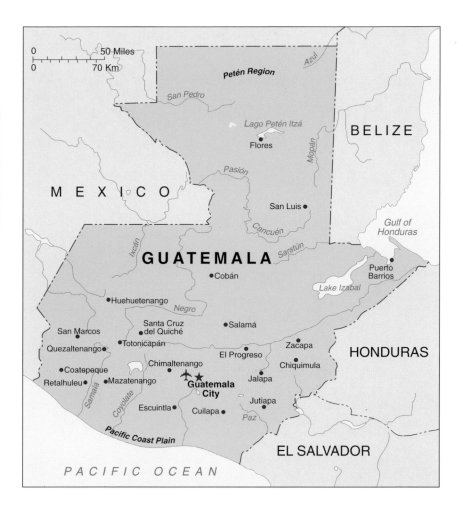

Guatemala's landscape is distinguished by three major land regions. The Petén region in the northeast is a flat, low, limestone **plateau** covered in tropical forests, which hide impressive Mayan ruins. Not many people inhabit this remote area, but the government is encouraging logging and new farming settlements—a plan Guatemalan conservation groups oppose.

Most of Guatemala's population live in the highlands in the southern half of the country. The climate there is cooler, and rainfall is moderate. Farmers grow coffee on the lower hillsides (up to about 5,000 feet) and plant maize and beans at the higher elevations. Cardamom, a valuable spice, is an important crop along the southern edge of the highlands. This region also contains the country's main urban centers, including the national capital, Guatemala City.

Guatemala's third region, the Pacific coastal plain, boasts fertile volcanic soil and an abundance of water tumbling from the Sierra Madre range. Coastal farmers produce fruits, vegetables, cotton, sugarcane, rice, and beef for both local use and export.

Cash-poor and heavily populated, Guatemala supplements its agriculturally based economy with the mining of oil, nickel, lead, and zinc. Industrial workers produce processed foods, clothing, textiles, and traditional crafts for export.

Huge stepped pyramids with wide, steep, stone stairways are typical of the Mayan ruins hidden in the forests of northern Guatemala's Petén region and Mexico's Yucatán Peninsula.

Honduras and El Salvador

Honduras

Status:	Republic
Area:	43,278 square miles
Population:	5.9 million
Capital:	Tegucigalpa
Languages:	Spanish, Indian languages
Currency:	Lempira (100 centavos)

Most of Honduras is mountainous, with several western peaks that rise to more than 8,000 feet. Oak and pine forests cover the foothills. Evergreen **cloud forests** grace the higher elevations. Nearly 60 percent of Hondurans live in small, scattered highland communities. Most are peasant farmers who own or rent small plots of land and produce just enough food for themselves, with a little extra to sell in local markets.

Narrow lowland plains run along the country's short Pacific coast and its longer Caribbean coast. Rich volcanic soil on the Pacific coastal plain supports large farms and cattle ranches. Farmers on the northern coast grow an abundance of bananas, which account for more than 30 percent of the country's exports. Honduras's only railroads snake through the northwestern coastal region, carrying bananas from the plantations to the port of Puerto Cortés. Coffee, sugarcane, beef, timber, and shrimp comprise the country's other major exports. Farmers grow maize and beans for local use.

Honduras has built few roads, and the interior of the country is largely undeveloped. Schools are few, especially in rural areas, and more than 40 percent of the population cannot read or write. About 15 percent of the people work in food processing, textile, furniture, and paper factories—industries situated in Tegucigalpa and San Pedro Sula, the country's two largest cities. Honduras abounds in minerals. Workers have mined only a small portion of the country's resources, such as silver, gold, lead, zinc, and cadmium.

Military dictators ruled Honduras for much of this century until 1981 when the Honduran people elected their first civilian government. It and the succeeding goverments have pledged to improve the country's living standards.

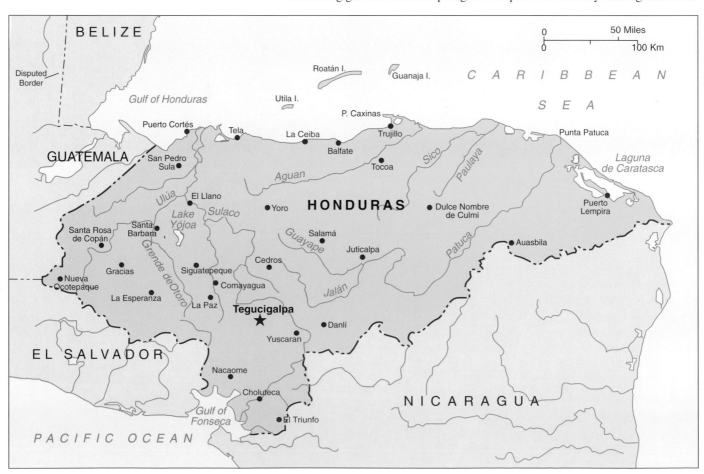

El Salvador

Status:	Republic
Area:	8,125 square miles
Population:	5.9 million
Capital:	San Salvador
Languages:	Spanish
Currency:	Colón (100 centavos)

El Salvador, the smallest of the Central American countries, has the third-largest population after Guatemala and Honduras. Nearly three-quarters of its people live in the country's central region—a wide rolling plateau with average temperatures of 73°F and about 45 inches of annual rain. Farms and ranches scattered across the plateau employ nearly half of El Salvador's workers. Small family farms grow beans, rice, maize, and other crops for home consumption and to sell at local markets. Many farmers also keep cows, pigs, and poultry. Most of the land belongs to large ranches raising beef and dairy cattle and to plantations of coffee—El Salvador's primary export crop. Plantations on the coastal plain grow sugarcane and cotton, which thrive in the hotter, wetter lowland climate. The Sierra Madre, a low mountain range created by ancient volcanic eruptions, forms El Salvador's northernmost boundary.

Most Salvadorans are mestizos (people of mixed Spanish and Indian ancestry), and the vast majority are poor. The wealthiest 2 percent of the population own most of the land in contrast to the nearly 20 percent who own none. This gulf between rich and poor led to a civil war that raged from 1980 to 1990. More than 75,000 people died, hundreds of thousands were left homeless, and the monetary drain on the country was enormous. Salvadorans are slowly rebuilding their country.

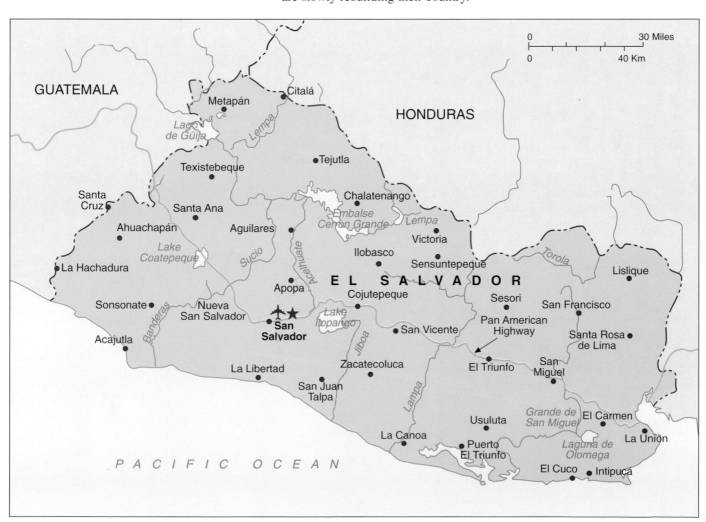

Nicaragua and Costa Rica

Nicaragua

Status:	Republic
Area:	50,193 square miles
Population:	5 million
Capital:	Managua
Language:	Spanish
Currency:	Gold córdoba (100 centavos)

Three distinct land regions divide Central America's largest country. The Pacific region consists of a fertile coastal plain, a range of hills and volcanoes, and a long depression containing Lake Nicaragua and Lake Managua—Central America's two largest lakes. The region enjoys a warm climate with ample rain from May to November. Local farmers cultivate cotton, sugarcane, and bananas for export and rice and vegetables for local consumption. The bulk of Nicaragua's people and industries inhabit this region, an area often hit by earthquakes. Seismic activity nearly destroyed the capital city of Managua in 1972.

The Central Highlands, although cooler than the Pacific region, also receive most of their rain between May and November. Highlanders primarily grow coffee—one of the country's major exports—and maize and beans for local consumption.

Nicaragua's third region is the flat, low-lying Caribbean coast where the climate is hot (average temperature of 80° F) and wet. More than 165 inches of rain fall each year in the dense tropical rain forest and coastal swamps and lagoons. Very few people live in this part of the country.

Nicaraguans recently endured one of Central America's most bitter civil wars. In 1979, the left-wing Sandinista movement forced from office their corrupt president, Anastasio Somoza. Right-wing Contras, supported by the United States, opposed the Sandinistas. After a decade of conflict, the two factions agreed to a cease-fire in 1989, but outbreaks of fighting continued until 1994 when the Sandinistas signed a peace agreement with the last of the Contras.

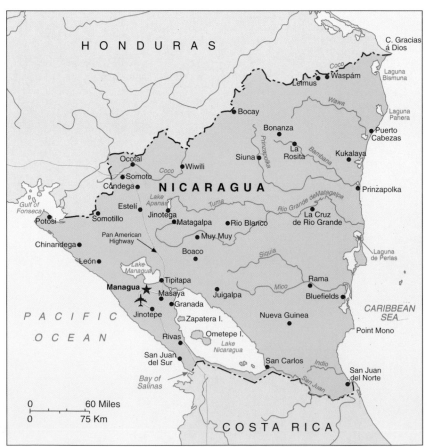

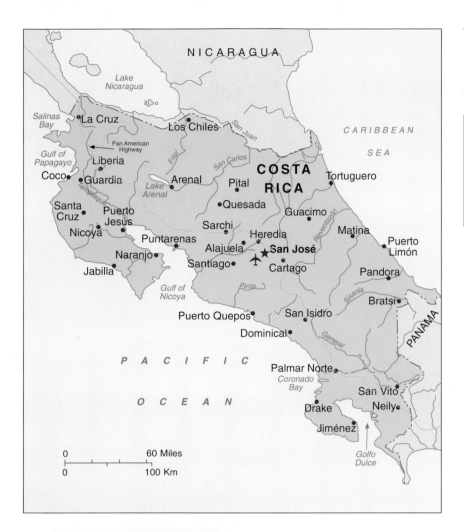

Costa Rica

Status:	Republic
Area:	19,730 square miles
Population:	3.6 million
Capital:	San José
Language:	Spanish
Currency:	Colón (100 centimos)

Costa Rica is a **republic** and one of the most stable countries in **Latin America.** The president and the 57 deputies of the Legislative Assembly are elected every four years, and all citizens 18 years of age or older are required to vote. Local government oversees such basic services as fire fighting and access to water supplies.

Most of Costa Rica's terrain is mountainous, and high plateaus run northwest to southeast across the country. These highlands contain two large areas of very fertile land, surrounded by rugged peaks. Roughly three-quarters of Costa Ricans live in the highlands, many of them employed by the coffee plantations that produce the country's second most significant **cash crop.** Highlanders also grow maize, cacao beans, rice, potatoes, and beans. To the west, a narrow coastal plain runs along the Pacific shore. The coastal climate is ideal for growing bananas, Costa Rica's major export. Coastal farmers supplement their banana crops with sugarcane and tropical fruits. The Caribbean Lowlands to the east are hot and humid, with some of the world's richest rain forest vegetation and wildlife. The coast alternates between swamps and forests and long sandy beaches.

Although Costa Rica depends largely on agriculture, the country also produces fertilizers, cement, machinery, furniture, cosmetics, and pharmaceuticals and enjoys a healthy tourism industry.

Coffee trees produce small white flowers and then bright red cherries that contain the coffee beans. Workers remove the soft flesh of the fruit and dry the beans in the sun before packing them for export.

Panama and the Canal

Panama

Status:	Republic
Area:	29,158 square miles
Population:	2.8 million
Capital:	Panama City
Languages:	Spanish, English
Currency:	Balboa (100 cents)

Narrow and S-shaped, Panama is the southernmost country on the isthmus linking North and South America. Bisected by the world's most famous canal, Panama is 450 miles long and 30 to 130 miles wide. Mountains run west to east across the country. The chain begins with Barú Volcano—an 11,400 feet peak near the border with Costa Rica—drops to the low rounded hills of the Canal Zone, and then rises again to 6,000 feet in the east. Very few people inhabit this forest-covered territory. More than 90 percent of the population lives in Panama's central region (near the canal) or on the Pacific coastal plain, where rich volcanic soil provides the country's most fertile farmland.

Panama City, at the canal's southern end, and Colón, at its northern end, are the country's largest cities and its centers of commerce and industry. Colón's Free Trade Zone allows companies to import and export goods without having to pay duties. Although not highly industrialized, Panama produces cement, beer, cigarettes, and processed foods. An oil refinery near Colón processes crude oil from other countries. Small farms grow **subsistence crops** of rice, maize, and beans. Larger farms and estates mass-produce bananas and other cash crops—sugarcane, coffee, and tobacco—for export to the United States and Europe.

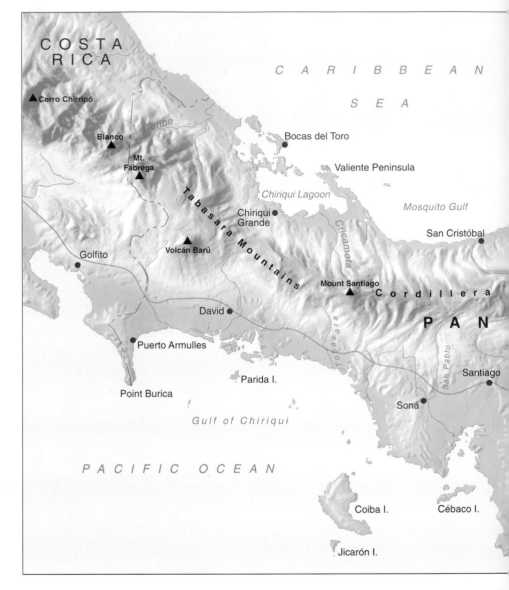

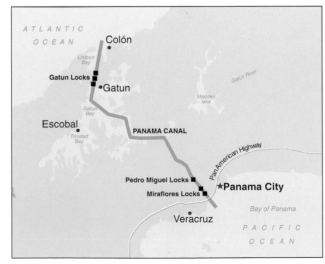

The Canal

The Panama Canal, which links the Atlantic Ocean with the Pacific Ocean, is one of the world's most significant waterways. Built by the United States between 1904 and 1914, the canal allows an average of 36 ships to pass through it each day, cutting thousands of miles from the long trip around South America. On the first stage of the 40-mile transit, a series of **locks** transports a ship 85 feet up to Gatun Lake. After crossing the lake, the ship enters the Gaillard Cut, a one-way channel just 160 yards wide that slices through the hills for more than eight miles. A second series of locks then lowers the ship to sea level again. After passing the city of Balboa, the ship sails under the Thatcher Ferry Bridge and heads into the Gulf of Panama.

A 1903 treaty between the United States and Panama allowed the United States to build the canal (at a cost of $380 million) and govern the Panama Canal Zone—a 10-mile-wide strip of land enveloping the canal. For years Panama tried to gain control of the canal and the Canal Zone. A treaty signed in 1977 returned territorial sovereignty of the Canal Zone to Panama in 1979 and gave Panama full operational control of the canal in 1999.

Left: Powerful electric locomotives running on tracks haul a cargo ship into one of the locks on the Panama Canal. Tugboats are used in addition to the locomotives when very large ships have to be maneuvered into place.

Right: This map shows just how important the canal is to ship operators. The 7 to 8 hour transit from the Pacific to the Atlantic saves 7,800 miles on a trip between New York and California—well worth the canal fee of about $30,000.

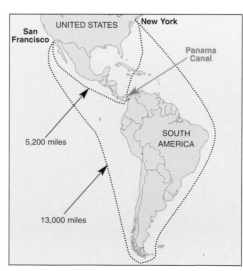

Colombia and Venezuela

Colombia

Status:	Republic
Area:	439,734 square miles
Population:	38.6 million
Capital:	Bogotá
Languages:	Spanish, Indian languages
Currency:	Peso (100 centavos)

Venezuela

Status:	Federal Republic
Area:	352,143 square miles
Population:	23.7 million
Capital:	Caracas
Languages:	Spanish
Currency:	Bolivar (100 céntimos)

Long coastlines on the Pacific Ocean and the Caribbean Sea cradle Colombia, South America's fourth-largest country. The rugged Andes Mountains dominate the western landscape, fanning across the country in three separate ranges. The Cauca and the Magdalena—Colombia's two largest rivers—flow through the valleys on either side of the central range. This vast highland region supports the country's richest farmland and many of its larger towns—Bogotá, Cali, Medellín, Armenia, and Manizales. Colombia's narrow Pacific coastal plain is swampy and wet with very few inhabitants. The Caribbean coast is quite busy by comparison because most of the country's exports pass through the ports of Santa Marta, Barranquilla, and Cartagena. East of the highlands, treeless grassy plains called **llanos** stretch nearly 500 miles to the Venezuelan border. Cattle ranching provides the most employment in this hot, dry region. Farther south the plains give way to the dense tropical rain forest of Amazonia.

Colombia produces more coffee than any other country except Brazil. Farmers also grow rice, potatoes, rubber, sugarcane, and bananas. Abundant coal reserves and massive oil production bolster the economy. Colombia is also rich in platinum and gold and produces 95 percent of the world's emeralds.

Most of Venezuela's people live in the highland regions of the north and northwest and on the narrow coastal plain. A vast llano lies between the northern mountains and the Orinoco River. South of the Orinoco, a mixture of savanna and forest covers the rest of the country, rising to the Guiana Highlands in the southeast. The climate varies from a dry north to a very wet south.

Venezuela is the largest oil producer in South America. Petroleum and refined petroleum products account for 94 percent of its exports. The country also has rich reserves of iron, bauxite (the source of aluminum), copper, nickel, manganese, gold, diamonds, and coal. Rivers provide hydroelectric power for the steel and aluminum industries. Venezuelans also process sugar and manufacture textiles, furniture, leather goods, paper, chemicals, and light machinery.

Venezuelan soil is not very fertile, so much of the land, especially the llanos, is used for cattle ranching. Rice, corn, sorghum, coffee, sugarcane, cotton, and tropical fruits are the major crops in more fertile areas. The country has untapped resources in its forests and coastal fisheries, and Venezuela's tourist trade is minimal, considering the country harbors the world's longest waterfall—the 3,212-foot Angel Falls in the Guiana Highlands.

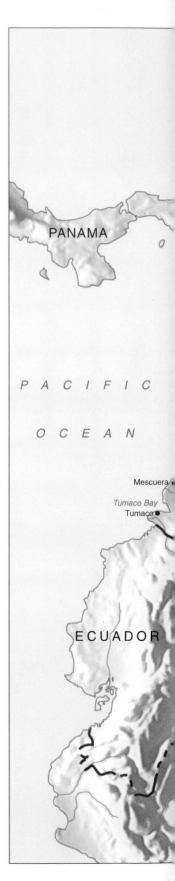

Music and dance play an important part in Colombian life, from the traditional songs and dances of rural villagers, like these members of a Bora Indian community, to the lavish carnivals of the big cities.

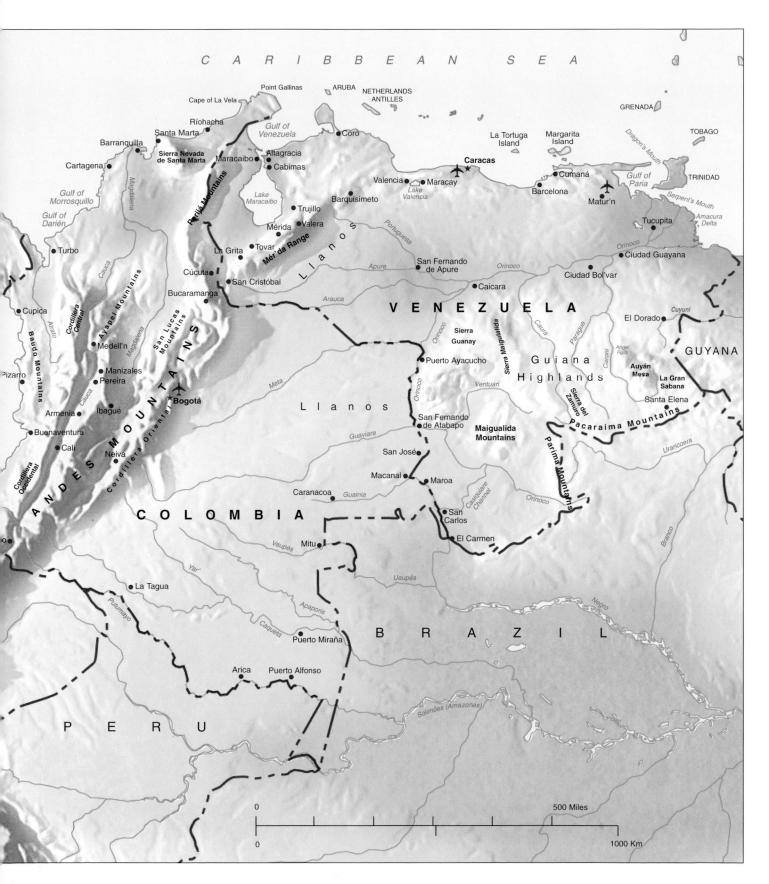

CARIBBEAN SEA

Point Gallinas
Cape of La Vela
ARUBA
NETHERLANDS
ANTILLES
GRENADA
TOBAGO

Ríohacha
Santa Marta
Coro
La Tortuga
Island
Margarita
Island

Barranquilla
Sierra Nevada
de Santa Marta
Maracaibo
Altagracia
Cabimas
Caracas
Cumaná
TRINIDAD

Cartagena
Gulf of
Venezuela
Valencia
Maracay
Barcelona
Gulf of
Paria

Gulf of
Morrosquillo
Lake
Maracaibo
Trujillo
Barquisimeto
Lake
Valencia
Matur'n

Gulf of
Darién
Mérida
Valera
Portuguesa
Tucupita

Turbo
La Grita
Tovar
Mér'da Range
Llanos
Amacura
Delta

Cupica
Cúcuta
San Cristóbal
Apure
San Fernando
de Apure
Orinoco
Ciudad Guayana

Pizarro
Bucaramanga
Arauca
Caicara
Ciudad Bol'var
Cuyuni

Medell'n
San Lucas
Mountains
VENEZUELA
El Dorado
GUYANA

Manizales
Pereira
Sierra
Guanay
G u i a n a
H i g h l a n d s
Auyán
Mesa
La Gran
Sabana

Armenia
Ibagué
Bogotá
Puerto Ayacucho
Santa Elena

Buenaventura
Neiva
L l a n o s
San Fernando
de Atabapo
**Maigualida
Mountains**
Pacaraima Mountains

Cali
Guaviare
San José
Macanal
Maroa
Orinoco

COLOMBIA
Caranacoa
Guainia
San
Carlos
Parima Mountains

Mitu
Vaupés
El Carmen
Casiquiare
Channel

Yar'
Uaupés

La Tagua
Putumayo
Apaporis
Caquetá
B R A Z I L
Negro

Puerto Miraña
Solimões (Amazonas)

Arica
Puerto Alfonso

P E R U

A N D E S   M O U N T A I N S
Cordillera Central
Ayapel Mountains
Cordillera Oriental
Cordillera Occidental
Baudo Mountains
Atrato
Cauca
Magdalena
Perijá Mountains

Sierra Maigualida
Caura
Paragua
Angel
Falls
Sierra del
Zamuro
Ventuari
Caroni
Uraricoera
Branco

0   500 Miles
0   1000 Km

17

Guyana, Suriname, French Guiana

Guyana

Status:	Republic
Area:	83,000 square miles
Population:	700,000
Capital:	Georgetown
Languages:	English, Asian languages, Amerindian languages
Currency:	Guyana dollar (100 cents)

Suriname

Status:	Republic
Area:	63,039 square miles
Population:	400,000
Capital:	Paramaribo
Languages:	Dutch, Sranan Tongo, English
Currency:	Suriname guilder (100 cents)

French Guiana

Status:	Overseas Department of France
Area:	34,749 square miles
Population:	200,000
Capital:	Cayenne
Languages:	French, local languages
Currency:	French franc (100 centimes)

These three locations on South America's northern coast have many similarities—hot, wet, tropical climates; average temperatures of 80°F; and average annual rainfall of 80 to 126 inches. Each has a narrow coastal plain, wherein lives the majority of the population. Savanna and woodlands merge into densely forested highlands farther inland.

Guyana began as a Dutch colony in 1581, coming under British control 250 years later (as British Guiana). The country gained independence in 1966 and became a republic in 1970. Most Guyanans are descended from African slaves and Asian laborers brought in to work the sugar plantations. The population also includes Europeans (mainly Portuguese) and Chinese. Guyana's economy depends entirely on exports. Sugarcane and bauxite each account for about 32 percent of the country's income, with rice, rum, gold, and diamonds comprising the balance.

Suriname, formerly Dutch Guiana, gained independence in 1975. Dutch is still the primary language, but people also speak English and a local **patois** called Taki-Taki. Children are required to attend school, and most of the population can read and write. Since the 1920s, Suriname has been the world's chief supplier of bauxite, but during the 1980s antigovernment guerrillas attacked the mines and processing plants, causing extensive damage. Farmers grow oil palms, rice, sugarcane, coffee, and tropical fruits on Suriname's fertile coastal plain. The government is helping to develop a fishing industry—primarily for shrimp.

French Guiana, an Overseas Department of France since 1946, has been under French rule since 1817. Most of the people are descendants of slaves brought to the territory in the 1600s and 1700s to work the sugarcane plantations. Later, the French built penal colonies, including the infamous Devil's Island offshore, to hold convicts sent from France. The country's economy is underdeveloped and depends on France for financial support. Guiana has iron, copper, silver, gold, lead, bauxite, and diamonds—but so far only gold is produced in any quantity. French Guiana is working with France to develop a shrimp fishing industry, and the country is also the site of the European Space Agency's launch facility.

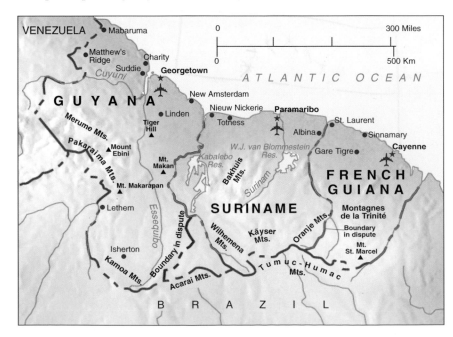

Mabaruma • Morawhaunna
Kaituma
Barima
IEZUELA
Cuyuni
Suddie •
Parika •
✈ ★ **Georgetown**
Arimu Mine •
Bartica •
Peters Mine •
Rosignol • New Amsterdam
Rockstone •
Linden •
Imbaimadai •
Issano •
Springlands
G U Y A N A
Demerara
Mazaruni
Ituni •
Berbice
Epira •
Potaro
Mahdia •
Orinduik •
Kurupukari •
SURINAME
Annai •
Good
Hope •
Apoteri •
Rupununi
Rewa
Essequibo
Lethem •
BRAZIL
Dadanawi •
Oronoque •
New
Isherton •
**CLAIMED BY
SURINAME**
Biloku •

0 ——— 80 Miles
0 ——— 130 Km
ATLANTIC
OCEAN

ATLANTIC
OCEAN
Les Hattes • • Mana
Saint-Laurent • Iracoubo
Saint-Jean • Sinnamary
Maroni
Apatou • Kourou •
Gare Tigre • Tonate •
Montainéry • ✈ ★ **Cayenne**
Saint-Elle • Roura •
Sinnamary
Mana
Comté
Abounamy
Kaw •
Grand Santi • Régina • Guisanbourg •
Bélizon •
*Oyapock
Bay*
Ouanary •
Patience • *Crique Arataye*
Cormontibo • Saint-Georges •
Approuague
SURINAME
Maripasoula • Saül •
**F R E N C H
G U I A N A**
Tampok
Canopi
Camopi •
Oyapock
CLAIMED BY SURINAME
Maroni
BRAZIL
Mt.
St. Marcel ▲

0 ——— 40 Miles
0 ——— 60 Km

Rockets launched toward the east from the European Space
Agency's facility at Kourou, French Guiana, gain a 1,500 feet-
per-second boost from the earth's spin.

ATLANTIC OCEAN
Nieuw
Nickerie • Totness • **Paramaribo** Nieuw
Jenny • ★ Amsterdam •
GUYANA
Nickerie
Groningen • Moengo •
Onverwacht • Lelydorp •
Zanderij ✈ • Albina •
Coppename
Apoera •
Bitagron •
Brokopondo •
Courantyne
Saramacca
Maroni
Bakhuis •
W.D.
Blommestein
Res.
**FRENCH
GUIANA**
*Wonotobo
Falls*
Pokigron •
Tapanahony
Surinam
*Tijer
Falls*
Kajana •
Cottica •
S U R I N A M E
Benzdorp •
Lucie
Apetina •
Anapaike •
Pelelu Tepu •
Paloemeu
Oleman
Litani
Area claimed
by Suriname
Kwamalasamutu •
BRAZIL

0 ——— 60 Miles
0 ——— 60 Km

Ecuador and the Galápagos Islands

Ecuador

Status:	Republic
Area:	109,483 sq. miles
Population:	12.4 million
Capital:	Quito
Languages:	Spanish, local Indian languages
Currency:	Sucre (100 centavos)

Spain ruled Ecuador from 1534 until 1822 and was responsible for many influences, including the country's name. Ecuador is Spanish for "equator"—the line of 0° latitude that runs across the country just north of the capital city of Quito.

Ecuador has three contrasting regions—a wide coastal plain, the mountains and high plateaus of the Andes, and an eastern lowland region sloping down into the Amazon Basin. The country also lays claim to the Galápagos Islands, which are located more than 600 miles to the west in the Pacific Ocean. Ecuador's coastal plain, 100 miles wide in places, supports a rich soil of mud and silt washed down from the Andes. The climate is hot and wet year-round. Plains farmers harvest bananas, coffee, and cacao beans for export from the port of Guayaquil and rice and sugarcane for local consumption. Coastal shrimp are another significant export.

Ecuador's Andean plateaus and valleys have a cooler, temperate climate ideal for cattle ranching and growing grains. The **haciendas** provide a much-needed paycheck for local citizens. Workers in the industrial cities of Quito, Ambato, Riobamba, and Cuenca produce textiles, shoes, and other leather goods. These cities lie on the **Pan-American Highway,** which runs from Santiago, Chile, to

the border between Mexico and the United States.

The eastern half of the country is covered in rain forest. This region is largely uninhabited, apart from small groups of Indians and the oil crews who are opening up the rich oil fields in the north. Oil has been Ecuador's most valuable export since the early 1970s. The country has become South America's second largest oil producer after Venezuela.

Thirteen volcanic islands and scores of rocks and reefs form the Galápagos Islands. Barren rock covers the shores, but dense forests blanket the inland mountains. The Galápagos Islands are famous for their unique animal life, including 500-pound giant tortoises and 5-foot-long marine iguanas. Naturalist Charles Darwin developed his theory of evolution after visiting the islands in 1835.

Galápagos Islands

Pinta

Marchena

Genovesa

Wolf Volcano

Darwin Volcano

Cumbre Volcano

San Salvador

▲Mt. Cowan

Alcedo Volcano

Fernandina

Rabida

Baltra

Isabela

Pinzón

Santa Rosa

▲Mt. Cooker

Cerro Azul Volcano

Santo Thomas

Puerto Ayora

Santa Cruz

San Cristóbal

Villamil

Santa Fé

▲Mt. San Joaquin

Tortuga

Baquerizo Moreno

0   25 Miles

0   40 Km

Santa María

Española

Ecuador

Galápagos Is.

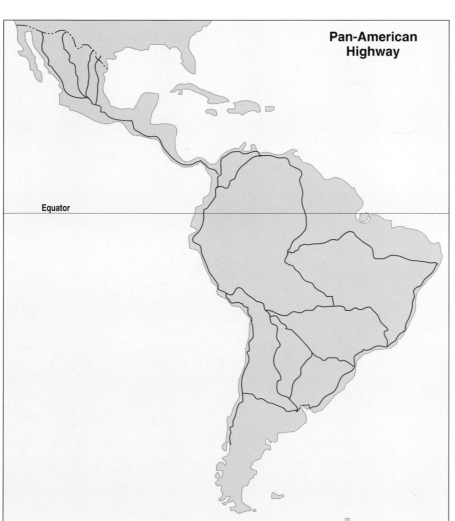

Pan-American Highway

Equator

Above: The marine iguana is just one of many unusual animals found on the Galápagos Islands. These prehistoric-looking creatures live on the rocky shores but feed on algae growing on rocks below sea level. The iguanas, giant tortoises, and unique birdlife of the islands inspired Charles Darwin's ideas on the evolution of life on earth.

Left: The Pan-American Highway runs from Santiago, in Chile, to the U.S. border with Mexico. Work started on the highway in 1936, and much of the work in Central America was financed by the United States. This amazing highway crosses deserts, plains, tropical rain forests, and 15,000-foot mountain passes.

Peru

Peru

Status:	Republic
Area:	496,224 square miles
Population:	26.6 million
Capital:	Lima
Languages:	Spanish, Quechua, Aymara
Currency:	Sol (100 cénts)

Andean villagers often sell handcrafted goods at the roadside. These women are selling decorative gourds, used to carry and drink water, and colorful handwoven clothes, rugs, and blankets.

South America's third-largest country enjoys a variety of climates and scenery. Peru's coastal plain is a 100-mile-wide strip of desert with patches of scrubby vegetation moistened only by winter fog that rolls in from the sea. Yet this barren plain is home to 45 percent of the population, to the country's capital, to its largest farms, and to its primary industries. Desert farmers produce cotton and sugarcane for export and rice, fruits, and vegetables for city markets. They irrigate farmland with water from mountain streams, a resource shared with people in nearby cities.

Peru's nearness to the ocean influences several areas of the local economy. Fishing crews catch vast quantities of sardines and anchovies each year. Most of the catch is processed into fish meal and exported as animal feed. The southern coast supports iron ore mining, and oil fields dot the northern coast. Peruvians even mine offshore islands for **guano** (manure used as fertilizer), which is exported from the chief port of Callao, near Lima.

Approximately 40 percent of the population lives in the Andes Mountains, where plateaus at 10,000 to 15,000 feet above sea level break around towering peaks of 21,000 feet. Fertile soil and a temperate climate enable farmers to grow coffee on the lower slopes and grains and potatoes on higher ground. Large flocks of sheep, alpacas, and llamas graze in the grassy valleys. Peruvian mountains are also rich in minerals. The country exports great quantities of copper, lead, silver, gold, and zinc.

Peru's eastern landscape consists of the lower slopes of the Andes and the Amazon Basin's rolling plain, all covered in dense rain forest. The area is inhabited primarily by small groups of native Indians.

Above: The Indians of the Peruvian highlands wear colorful traditional costumes of handwoven cloth made from the wool of llamas, alpacas, and guanacos. Warm clothing, a thick shawl, and an embroidered cap keep this young girl warm despite the cold of the high mountains.

Left: Visitors travel from around the world to marvel at the ruins of Machu Picchu, an ancient Incan settlement perched above the Urubamba Valley, 7,875 feet up in the Peruvian Andes. The site is famous for its fine architecture and the terraced fields on the steep surrounding hillsides. Machu Picchu was discovered in 1911 by the American archaeologist Hiram Bingham.

Brazil

Brazil

Status:	Federal Republic
Area:	3.3 million square miles
Population:	168 million
Capital:	Brasília
Language:	Portuguese
Currency:	Real
	(100 centavos)

Brazil encompasses nearly half of the continent, sharing borders with every other South American country except Chile and Ecuador. Nearly as large as the United States, Brazil has far fewer people and much of its interior is uninhabited.

Northern Brazil consists of the vast Amazon Basin, which is bordered by the Guiana Highlands in the north and the Andes in the west. This huge area of hills and plains is warm and wet year-round. Covered by the world's largest tropical rain forest, northern Brazil embraces the world's greatest river system—the Amazon and its main tributaries, which flow for nearly 4,000 miles from the Andes to the Atlantic Ocean. The river is so big and so deep that oceangoing ships can easily navigate it for more than 1,000 miles inland.

The southern half of the country consists of the Brazilian Highlands—on of high plateaus and deep valleys. The climate is seasonal.

Above: Carnival time in Rio de Janeiro is one of the noisiest and most colorful spectacles in the world.

Left: Iguazú Falls, on the border between Brazil and Argentina, consist of 275 separate waterfalls plunging 280 feet from a 2.5-mile-wide **escarpment**.

Below: Enormous open-pit iron ore mines scar the landscape at Belo Horizonte in the Minas Gerais province of southeastern Brazil.

Brazil

The south has cool winters and rain-drenched summers, perfect for the treeless savanna. Farmers graze cattle and sheep at the higher elevations and farm the fertile valleys and coastal plains. Roughly 80 percent of Brazil's population lives within 200 miles of the Atlantic coast. São Paulo, Rio de Janeiro, Salvador, and Recife—Brazil's major cities—lie on the country's southeastern coast.

Brazil produces more crops, timber, minerals, and manufactured goods than any other country in South America. Major commercial crops are coffee, cacao beans, soybeans, bananas, tobacco, sugarcane, maize, and oranges. Brazil raises beef cattle, horses, pigs, and sheep. The country is one of the world's chief exporters of iron ore, bauxite, beryllium, chrome, tin, manganese, magnesium, gold, and diamonds. Oil and gas wells along the coast produce fuel, as well as the raw materials for the country's petro-chemical industries. Brazil is the most heavily industrialized country in South America, and its exports include cars, aircraft, textiles, cement, chemicals, electrical goods, ma-chinery, and paper.

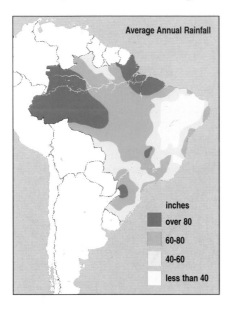

Average Annual Rainfall

inches

- over 80
- 60-80
- 40-60
- less than 40

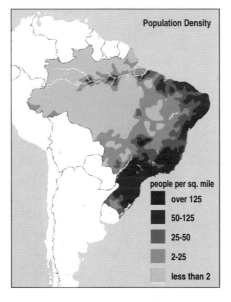

Population Density

people per sq. mile

- over 125
- 50-125
- 25-50
- 2-25
- less than 2

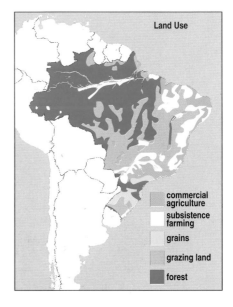

Land Use

- commercial agriculture
- subsistence farming
- grains
- grazing land
- forest

Right: The National Congress is one of many stunning modern buildings in the capital, Brasília, 3,500 feet above sea level on the central plateau. Work started on the city in 1957, and the government moved there from Rio de Janeiro in 1960.

Bolivia

Bolivia

Status:	Republic
Area:	424,162 sq. miles
Population:	8.1 million
Capital:	La Paz
Languages:	Spanish, Aymara, Quechua
Currency:	Boliviano (100 centavos)

Above: The Cathedral of San Francisco overlooks this busy square in the Bolivian capital of La Paz. La Paz was founded by the Spanish in 1548, on the route between the Potosi silver mines and the port at Lima on the coast of Peru. At 12,000 feet above sea level, La Paz is the highest capital city in the world.

Bolivia, like many of its South American neighbors, has three contrasting regions. The high plateaus of the **altiplano** dominate the west, surrounded by the snow-covered peaks of the Andes. The highland climate is cold and dry, with nighttime temperatures often falling below freezing. Despite the harsh conditions, most Bolivians live in this area. Herders raise llamas and alpacas for their wool on the sparse grasslands of the highlands. In the more fertile areas—around Lake Titicaca and the cities of Cochabamba and Sucre—farmers grow potatoes, maize, quinoa, wheat, and oca, an edible tuber. Coffee, cacao beans, beans, rice, cotton, and fruits comprise the major crops in the eastern lowlands.

The climate is humid in northern Bolivia where dense forests merge with the Amazon rain forest. Southern and central Bolivia enjoy gentle hills and wide valleys, and in the southeast, semi-arid grasslands merge with the **Gran Chaco** of Paraguay. Ranchers raise cattle on the drier plains. Nearly half of Bolivia's workers are employed as farm laborers, but the country is very poor, barely producing enough food for its own needs. Peasant farmers in many areas illegally grow coca, the source of cocaine.

Mines in the altiplano produce tin, copper, lead, tungsten, silver, and zinc. Large oil fields and natural gas fields lie beneath the eastern plains. Hydroelectric power stations on major rivers produce energy for the country's industries. Bolivia's principal exports are minerals (chiefly tin), natural gas, and textiles. The goods are shipped overland by road through Chile and Peru or south by river through Paraguay.

Paraguay and Uruguay

Paraguay

Status:	Republic
Area:	157,046 sq. miles
Population:	5.2 million
Capital:	Asunción
Languages:	Spanish, Guarani
Currency:	Guarani (100 céntimos)

The Paraguay River divides this landlocked country in two. A vast plain lies to the west of the river, rising gently from marshy bottomland near the river to the semi-arid Gran Chaco in Paraguay's northwest. Chaco vegetation is a mixture of coarse grasses, cacti, and thorny scrub—land best used for grazing cattle. A region of higher land lies east of the river, with alternating areas of grassland and hardwood forest. About 90 percent of Paraguayans live in this fertile eastern area. In addition to raising livestock, farmers grow maize, cassava, rice, and sugarcane for local use and tobacco, soybeans, and cotton for export.

Because Paraguay lacks a coast, the country's exports are shipped down the Paraguay River and on to the Atlantic Ocean, 1,000 miles away. The river, however, is so deep that 1,700-ton ships are able to sail upriver as far as the capital of Asunción.

Paraguay's chief energy source is hydroelectricity. And the country produces enough to export some to its neighbors. The gigantic Itaipu Dam on the Paraná River, built in partnership with Brazil, is the world's largest hydroelectric installation. With Argentina's help, Paraguay is nearing completion on a second huge hydroelectric plant at Yacyreta.

High-quality tropical hardwoods are one of Paraguay's most valuable natural resources. Tree species harvested include the quebracho, a source of tannin used to tan hides for leather.

Uruguay

Status:	Republic
Area:	68,498 sq. miles
Population:	3.4 million
Capital:	Montevideo
Language:	Spanish
Currency:	Uruguayan peso (100 centésimos)

Uruguay, one of South America's smallest countries, is dwarfed by its neighbors, Brazil and Argentina. Its landscape consists of gently rolling long-grass prairies with ribbons of woodland growing alongside its rivers. Uruguay's highest point is just 1,640 feet above sea level. The climate is temperate, with warm summers and cool winters. Rain falls throughout the year. The country's many large rivers provide plenty of hydroelectric power, and the Paso de los Toros on the Río Negro has created the largest artificial lake in South America—the Embalse del Río Negro reservoir.

Uruguay's grasslands are ideal for grazing livestock. Local ranchers raise about 10 million cattle and 20 million sheep. Beef, wool, and leather goods are some of the country's main exports. The fertile soil of Uruguay's coastal plains supports a diversity of agriculture—wheat, rice, sorghum, maize, potatoes, and sugar beets—as well as milk and dairy products for the home market.

Most Uruguayans live in the coastal region—about half of them in the capital of Montevideo and the surrounding area. Beautiful beaches have helped boost tourism, a vital source of jobs and income. Uruguay has no mineral wealth, so machinery, cars and trucks, chemicals, and many other goods must be imported.

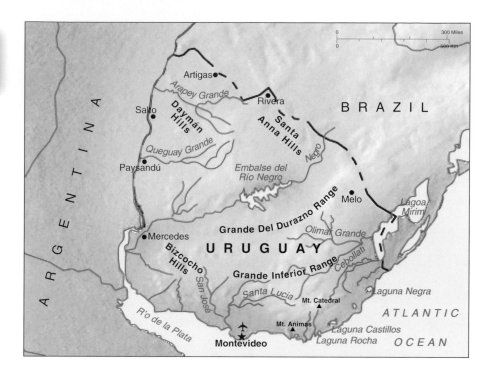

Well-developed educational, health, and welfare systems help Uruguay remain one of the most stable Latin American countries, despite some political unrest.

Chile

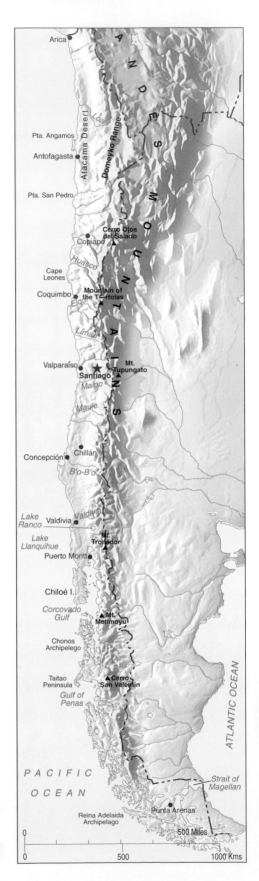

Chile

Status:	Republic
Area:	292,135 square miles
Population:	15 million
Capital:	Santiago
Language:	Spanish
Currency:	Peso (100 centavos)

Chile is one of the world's most unusual countries in shape and climate. A narrow strip of land extending 2,600 miles from north to south, Chile's green bean shape averages only 110 miles wide. The country's northernmost point is well inside the **tropics** and yet contains one of the driest deserts on earth. Far to the south, Chile's Cape Horn lies at the tip of Tierra del Fuego and is a land of forests, glaciers, and rocky mountain peaks jutting into the wild Southern Ocean. The country's narrow width slivers into three contrasting landscapes. Steep, rocky cliffs dominate the western coastline. Just inland lies a fertile central valley—

home to most of the country's population, agriculture, and industry. The Andes Mountains rise steeply in the east, separating Chile from neighboring Argentina and Bolivia.

Chile enjoys one of South America's strongest economies, relying primarily on its significant mineral resources. The country is one of the world's chief producers of copper, and it also has large reserves of iron ore, lead, zinc, gold, silver, iodine, sulfur, and borax. Chile is one of the few South American countries with large coal deposits, although hydroelectric power and oil account for most of the country's energy supplies. Timber, manufactured goods, fruits and vegetables, fish, and by-products such as fish oil and fish meal also contribute to the local economy.

From 1973 to 1990, Chile was ruled by a military **junta** led by General Augusto Pinochet. In 1990 the country returned to democratically elected government, with a 120-member Chamber of Deputies and a 38-member Senate. Since the mid-1960s, all Chilean schoolchildren have had access to free primary education, and the country has one of the highest literacy rates in Latin America.

Above: An oil production platform sits off Punta Arenas in southern Chile. The oil fields in this region produce about half the country's fuel needs.

Left: Torres del Paine National Park in the Chilean Andes contains some of the finest scenery—and most demanding mountain climbing—in the entire Andes range.

Right: Significant resources of both metallic and nonmetallic ores, plus coal, oil, and hydroelectric power, make Chile one of the world's leading exporters of minerals.

Argentina

Argentina

Status:	Republic
Area:	1.07 million sq. miles
Population:	36.6 million
Capital:	Buenos Aires
Language:	Spanish
Currency:	Peso
	(100 australes)

South America's second-largest country is more than 2,170 miles long from north to south and 870 miles across at its widest point. Nestling into Chile's curved eastern border, Argentina covers most of the southern part of the continent. A varied landscape begins in the west with the Andes Mountains, whose highest peak, Aconcagua, towers over the region at 22,831 feet. The chaco in the northeast is damp and subtropical, with forested plains and swampy areas. The bulk of the country east of the Andes consists of rolling lowland plains. Flat and fertile, the **pampas** blanket most of eastern and central Argentina, from the dry west to the humid east where moist winds blow in from the Atlantic. South of the pampas lies the dry, windswept region of Patagonia and beyond that are the low mountains of the southern Andes and Tierra del Fuego, with their snowcapped peaks, ice fields, and glaciers.

Argentina's pampas boast large areas of fertile soil, a necessity for the country's agriculturally based economy. Farmers in the moist temperate regions produce wheat, maize, rye, soybeans, and linseed for export and fruit and vegetables for home consumption. In the drier regions, gauchos (cowboys) manage vast herds of beef cattle. Meat packing and food processing are primary industries, but Argentina also produces cars and trucks, iron and steel, cement, chemicals, textiles, and petroleum products. The country has few mineral resources apart from coal, iron ore, and uranium. Hydroelectricity provides about half of the country's energy. Coal and petroleum supply the rest. Locally mined uranium could be used for fuel rods should the country decide to use nuclear energy. Pine, larch, and oak forests in the flatland of Patagonia provide valuable timber for both local use and export, and Argentina's fishing crews catch hake, mackerel, anchovies, tuna, and squid.

Good schools and excellent medical services allow Argentinians to enjoy one of the highest standards of living in South America.

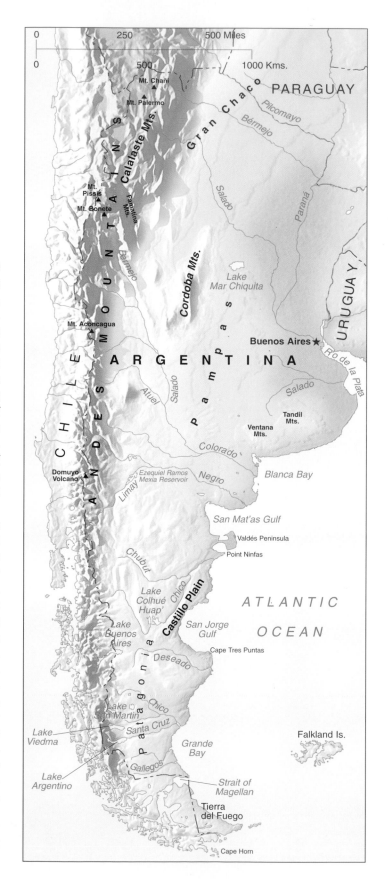

Top: Like cowboys everywhere, the gauchos of the Argentinian pampas enjoy showing off their skill with horses.

Above: Buenos Aires—the capital and main cultural, business, and industrial center—has a population of about 3 million. More than 10 million people inhabit the metropolitan district. The residents proudly call themselves *portenos*, which means "people of the port."

Atlantic Islands

The vast Atlantic Ocean is home to less than 100 islands, relatively few compared to the Pacific Ocean. Large islands lie close to the mainland. Smaller islands, most of them the tops of submarine volcanoes (some extinct, some still active), rise from the **Mid-Atlantic Ridge**. The islands are rugged and mountainous, with steep slopes ending in sheer sea cliffs. People who inhabit these remote islands make their living primarily from subsistence farming, fishing, and tourism—the Azores, Madeira, Canary, and Cape Verde Islands entertain many foreign visitors each year. Cape Verde in the North Atlantic is an important refueling stop for transatlantic ships and aircraft, and Ascension Island in the South Atlantic has a U.S. military base and a satellite tracking station. Most of these islands are overseas territories of Britain, Spain, and Portugal, and they rely financially on their parent countries for the essentials such as food and fuel. Cape Verde is an independent nation, which receives financial help from international aid organizations and from Cape Verdians who work abroad.

The Falkland Islands, 320 miles east of South America, rise from the South American continental shelf, rather than from the deep ocean floor. Low and windswept, the Falklands are covered in tussock grass and peat bogs. Islanders raise sheep for their livelihood. Mineral resources in the surrounding seas could also supplement the island's economy, but the industry has not yet been developed. Both Argentina and Great Britain claim ownership of this island group.

Madeira

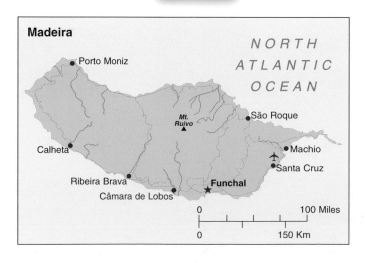

The Azores

Status:	Self-governing Region of Portugal
Area:	880 square miles
Population:	238,000
Capital:	Ponta Delgada
Language:	Portuguese
Currency:	Portuguese escudo (100 centavos)

The group consists of nine main islands spread over 400 miles of the eastern Atlantic. The Azores are rugged, with a temperate climate. Farmers grow bananas and subtropical fruits at the lower elevations and grains and temperate fruits higher up. Islanders fish for tuna and sardines to export. The islands also have a growing tourist industry.

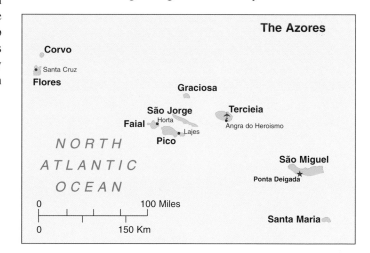

Status:	Self-governing Region of Portugal
Area:	315 square miles
Population:	270,000
Capital:	Funchal
Language:	Portuguese
Currency:	Portuguese escudo (100 centavos)

A warm, temperate climate and rich soil allow the islanders to grow sugarcane, vines, and both temperate and tropical fruits and vegetables. Grapes from the island's vineyards are processed into Madeira wine, a very popular export. Tourism is an important and growing industry.

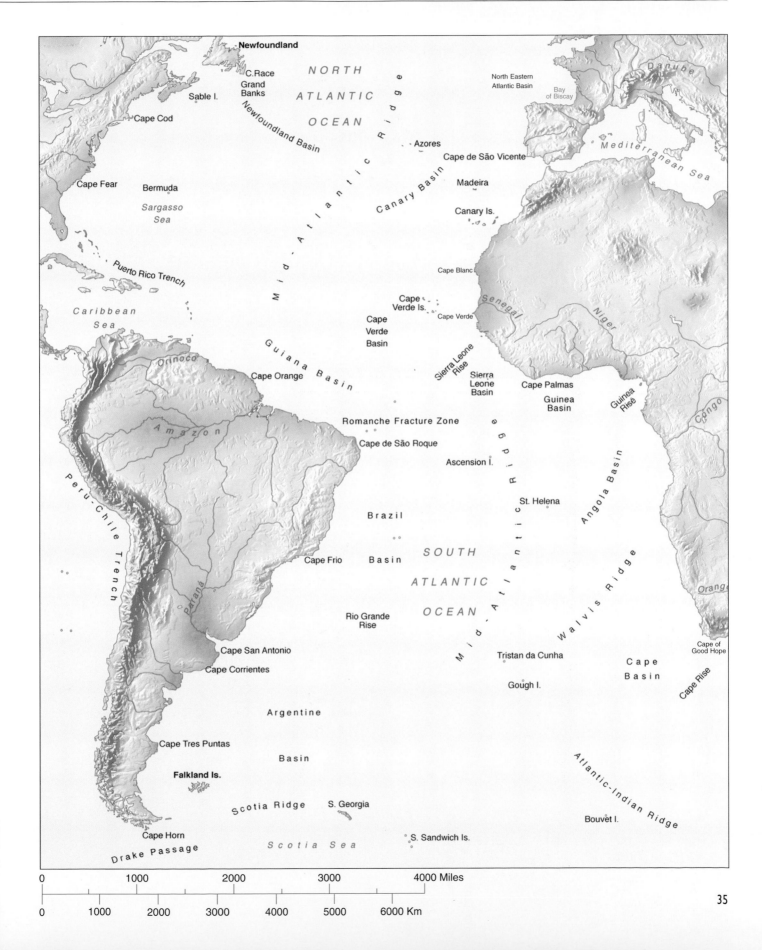

Newfoundland

C. Race
Grand
Banks

Sable I.

NORTH
ATLANTIC
OCEAN

Cape Cod

Newfoundland Basin

North Eastern
Atlantic Basin

Bay
of Biscay

Danube

Azores

Cape de São Vicente

Mediterranean Sea

Cape Fear

Bermuda

Sargasso
Sea

Canary Basin

Madeira

Canary Is.

Mid-Atlantic Ridge

Puerto Rico Trench

Cape Blanc

Senegal

Niger

Caribbean
Sea

Cape
Verde Is.

Cape
Verde
Basin

Cape Verde

Orinoco

Cape Orange

Guiana Basin

Sierra Leone
Rise

Sierra
Leone
Basin

Cape Palmas

Congo

Amazon

Romanche Fracture Zone

Guinea
Basin

Guinea
Rise

Cape de São Roque

Ascension Í.

Mid-Atlantic Ridge

Peru-Chile Trench

Brazil

St. Helena

Angola Basin

Basin

SOUTH

Cape Frio

ATLANTIC

Parana

OCEAN

Rio Grande
Rise

Mid-Atlantic Ridge

Walvis Ridge

Orange

Cape San Antonio

Cape Corrientes

Tristan da Cunha

C a p e
B a s i n

Cape of
Good Hope

Gough I.

Cape Rise

Argentine

Cape Tres Puntas

Basin

Atlantic-Indian Ridge

Falkland Is.

Scotia Ridge

S. Georgia

Bouvet I.

Cape Horn

Scotia Sea

S. Sandwich Is.

Drake Passage

0		1000		2000		3000		4000 Miles

0	1000	2000	3000	4000	5000	6000 Km

Atlantic Islands

Canary Islands

Status:	Self-governing Region of Spain
Area:	2,800 square miles
Population:	1.5 million
Capital:	Las Palmas
Language:	Spanish
Currency:	Peseta (100 centimos)

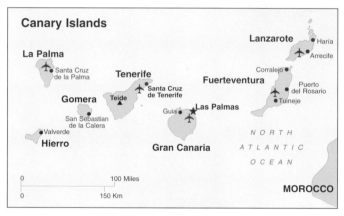

Above: The lowland and coastal areas of Tenerife are lush and fertile, but the island's mountainous interior is wild and rugged. Wind and rain have carved this rock pillar, standing like a sentry on the approach to Pico de Teide volcano.

Most of the islands in this group are rugged and mountainous. Only Lanzarote and Fuerteventura, nearest the African coast, are flat. Pico de Teide volcano on Tenerife erupted in 1909 and towers over the area at 12,156 feet. Fertile soil and irrigation procedures allow farmers to grow sugarcane, coffee, and tropical fruits on low ground and grains and temperate vegetables at the higher elevations. Tourism flourishes on the main islands.

Cape Verde Islands

Status:	Republic
Area:	1,556 square miles
Population:	400,000
Capital:	Praia
Language:	Portuguese
Currency:	Cape Verde escudo (100 centavos)

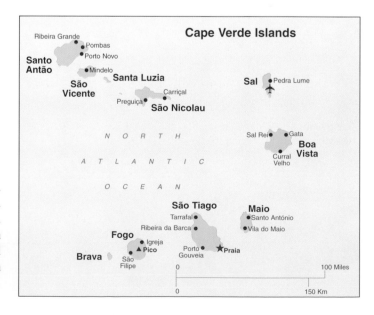

The islands are volcanic, mountainous, and very rugged. Cano Peak on Fogo Island is the highest point at 9,281 feet. The climate is arid, and much of the land is badly eroded. Local farmers grow maize, vegetables, and some fruits on land that has been improved by irrigation and by soil conservation programs. The islands' main exports are rum and fish (mainly tuna and lobster).

Falkland Islands

Status:	Overseas Territory of Great Britain
Area:	4,700 square miles
Population:	2,120
Capital:	Stanley
Language:	English
Currency:	Pound (100 pence)

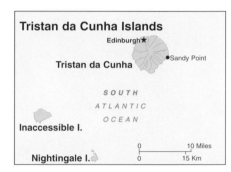

Falkland Islands

The Falklands consist of two main islands and nearly 200 smaller islands and islets. About half the population lives in the capital, Stanley. The remainder inhabits the outlying sheep stations. Since the war with Argentina in 1982, Britain has maintained a military garrison and air base on the islands.

Saint Helena Island

Status:	Overseas Territory of Great Britain
Area:	47 square miles
Population:	6,700
Capital:	Jamestown
Language:	English
Currency:	Pound (100 pence)

This mountainous island, 1,200 miles from the coast of Africa, is famous as the place where Napoléon Bonaparte died in exile in 1821. The island's small population lives by farming and by creating lace and flax for export. Saint Helena is the administrative center for several smaller British Overseas Territories, including Ascension Island and Tristan da Cunha.

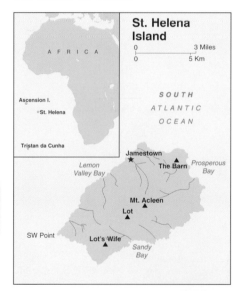

St. Helena Island

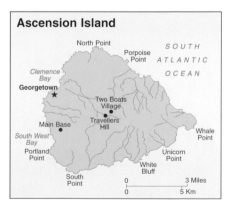

Tristan da Cunha Islands

Tristan da Cunha Islands

Status:	Overseas Territory of Great Britain
Area:	40 square miles
Population:	330
Capital:	Edinburgh
Language:	English
Currency:	Pound (100 pence)

Ascension Island

Status:	Overseas Territory of Great Britain
Area:	34 square miles
Population:	1,200
Capital:	Georgetown
Language:	English
Currency:	Pound (100 pence)

Ascension Island

The largest of these remote volcanic islands, Tristan da Cunha sits at the southern end of the Mid-Atlantic Ridge. The climate is mild and wet. Islanders grow vegetables and raise sheep and cattle. The entire population was evacuated in 1961 when a volcano erupted. Most returned in 1963.

More than 700 miles northwest of Saint Helena, Ascension Island is most famous for the sea turtles that lay their eggs on its beaches each year. The inhabitants are mainly British and American. Many of them work at the satellite tracking station and the military airfield.

Glossary

altiplano: a region of high plateaus in the Andean region of South America

cash crop: a crop that is produced mainly to make money and not to feed one's family

cloud forest: a forest that is located in mountainous areas of the tropics, where heavy mists occur

coral reef: a ridge of rocklike formations made of billions of coral polyp skeletons

escarpment: an inland cliff or steep slope

federation: a form of government in which states or groups unite under a central power. The states or groups surrender power to make some decisions but retain limited territorial control.

foreign exchange: deposits of foreign money or short-term credit instruments that enable countries to do business

Gran Chaco: a sparsely inhabited wilderness area in northern Paraguay that is swampy in the rainy season and parched in the dry season

guano: a substance formed mainly of the excrement (body wastes) of birds or bats. The substance is valued as a fertilizer.

hacienda: a large estate or plantation in a Spanish-speaking country

isthmus: a narrow strip of land connecting two large land areas

junta: a group of military people who put themselves in power after overthrowing a government

Latin America: a group of countries in Central America, South America, and the Caribbean in which the main language is Spanish, Portuguese, or French

llanos: the vast tropical grasslands in the Orinoco Basin and the Guiana Highlands

lock: an enclosed, water-filled chamber in a canal used to raise or lower boats from one water level to another

Mid-Atlantic Ridge: the north-south ridge that rises from the ocean floor. It runs more or less parallel to the continental coastlines on either side of the Atlantic Ocean. The tips of the ridge that break the ocean's surface are the Atlantic Islands.

pampas: a region of grassy plains in Argentina. The western pampas are dry and largely desert. The eastern pampas support coarse grasses and cultivated plants suitable for grazing large herds of cattle and sheep.

Pan-American Highway: an international highway system in the Americas

patois: a local form of language that is different from the standard form

plateau: a large, relatively flat area that stands above the surrounding land

republic: a government having a chief of state (usually a president) who is not a monarch. In a republic, supreme power belongs to a body of citizens who are entitled to vote and who elect representatives responsible to the citizens. These representatives govern according to law.

savanna: a tropical grassland where annual rainfall varies from season to season

sovereign state: a country that is independent and exercises control over its own territory

subsistence crop: a crop that is produced mainly to feed one's family with little, if any, surplus for market

tropics: the hot, wet region that forms a wide belt around the earth's equator between the Tropic of Cancer and the Tropic of Capricorn

Index